SATAN'S WAR AGAINST THE GODHEAD

STEVE WOHLBERG

Present Truth Publications
Priest River, Idaho 83856

Photography and cover design by Jaime Galvez

Copyright © Present Truth Publications

Printed in the United States of America
All rights reserved

The author assumes full responsibility for the accuracy of all facts and quotations as cited in this book.

All scripture verses taken from the New King James Version (NKJV), except where indicated as the King James Version (KJV), which is in the public domain.

New King James Version®. Copyright © 1982 by Thomas Nelson. Used by permission. All rights reserved.

You can obtain additional copies of this book by calling toll-free 1-800-765-6955 or by visiting AdventistBookCenter.com.

Library of Congress Cataloging-in-Publication Data

ISBN: 979-8-9887560-1-9

First printing: October 2023

DEDICATED TO
THE FATHER,
THE SON, AND
THE HOLY SPIRIT

CONTENTS

WHAT READERS ARE SAYING

The book you hold in your hand is both simple and profound. It places the full weight of its teaching on inspired writings, making it not only a must-read for every Seventh-day Adventist but also an important read for every Christian. For those who have wrestled with the issue of the Godhead, this book will deliver. Short, to the point, and yet exhaustive enough to cover the topic, Pastor Steve Wohlberg takes in all the main points and issues before us regarding this challenging truth. Answers, answers, answers, in a clear and understandable manner, is what readers will discover in *Satan's War Against the Godhead.* When you're finished, you will also see more clearly the importance of not being endlessly distracted by these issues and

moving forward to present a unified Three Angels' message to a lost and dying world.
—Pastor James Rafferty, 3ABN Director of Discipleship

"The most solemn truths ever entrusted to mortals" have been given to God's end-time remnant church, and "the proclamation of these truths is our work." *Counsels on Stewardship*, p. 38. One of the most effective strategies of the enemy in warring against the Godhead and God's church is to create distractions and division among the Lord's people. The degree to which this strategy is successful is dependent on the extent to which God's people stray from *Sola Scriptura* and venture into mere human opinions. By adhering to Inspiration and avoiding speculation, Pastor Steve brings clarity to a topic that has unnecessarily divided churches and led many to leave the fold of the remnant. In *Satan's War Against the Godhead*, Pastor Steve unveils this satanic strategy, and reveals how some in the church today are, perhaps unwittingly, continuing the enemy's work of bringing confusion and division through teachings that are now distracting Adventists from our mission. I believe the Holy

Spirit will use this timely book to help bring harmony among God's people on these issues and the unity He so desires for His people (1 Cor. 1:10)—a unity that is modeled by the Heavenly Trio.—Rob Durkin (www .theheavenlytrio.com)

Satan's War Against the Godhead is an important book. Interestingly written, it tackles the subject of the mystery of the Godhead in a reverent way. This mystery is a topic that Lucifer successfully used to deceive the angels in heaven. Through the millennia he has continued to use arguments about God to deceive mankind. Though we can never fully understand the mystery of divinity, God has revealed enough about Himself to keep us from accepting Satan's false theories. Drawing from the Bible, Spirit of Prophecy, and personal experience, the author uses the inspired writings to answer basic questions. He addresses with careful detail the confusing and sometimes twisted Bible and Spirit of Prophecy passages. This book reviews the progress of truth through the 1888 message. It analyzes historical items of significance such as the Kellogg crisis and its attack on a true understanding of divinity. I am glad to have this valuable resource, not only for myself, but to share with friends who have been confronted and sometimes confused by subtle arguments about the Godhead.—Phil Mills, MD

Satan's War Against the Godhead reveals a different perspective from any book I have read on this topic. It not only covers real issues such as the "One True God" movement but also why church organization and pressing together are so important as we near the end of time. Excellent book!—Linda Brehm

I am so grateful to God for placing the burden on Steve's heart to write this timely and critically important work. Satan is the father of lies, and his old errors regarding the Godhead are being repackaged today and find surprising traction even within God's Remnant Church. Steve does a great job showing how these errors are tied together and why it really does matter what you believe about the Godhead, especially as we near the end of time. May God give light to His people through this book.—John Krum

Author's Introduction

Most of my books have been written to teach biblical truths to the general public, but a few have been written specifically for members of my own denomination—the Seventh-day Adventist Church. This is one of those books. This doesn't mean that those who aren't Adventists shouldn't read it, or that they can't be richly blessed by the biblical truths explained here. Not at all. In fact, every person on earth needs to understand what lies within these pages. But it does mean that this particular work, while based solidly on God's Word, also explores some unique twists, turns, and controversies now taking place among Adventists as a distinct people.

The fact that many Adventists are wrestling with some controversial issues, too, shouldn't surprise us, simply because the fierce battle between Satan and his rebel angels against Jesus Christ and His loyal angels has been raging throughout history, in every land, in every church, and in every heart.

It is raging today.

This book is about *that war.*

Shortly before ascending to heaven (see Acts 1:9–11), our Savior gave His Great Commission to His followers:

Go therefore and make disciples of all the nations, baptizing them in the name of the Father and of the Son and of the Holy Spirit. Matthew 28:19

From this Great Commission we learn that:

1. Jesus told His church to *"Go"* and "make disciples of all nations." Nothing should be allowed to distract or deter us from fulfilling this commission.

2. Those who "Go" to "all nations" are to baptize "in the name of *the Father and of the Son and of the Holy Spirit."* This implies that people living among "all nations" should be taught about the Father, the Son, and the Holy Spirit.

3. These words also reveal that there IS a Father (*"the* Father"), a Son (*"the* Son"), and a Holy Spirit (*"the* Holy Spirit").

Satan and his evil angels are fiercely opposed to our going, teaching, and baptizing. Instead, they would rather have us stop, sit, argue, and debate—especially about the nature of the Father, the Son, and the Holy Spirit. Four major goals of this book are:

1. To counteract Satan's efforts.

2. To clarify what we know about the Godhead.

3. To bring God's people closer together in unity.

4. To focus our minds on Jesus Christ, His love, and on His commission that we "Go," rather than sit and debate.

The last book of the Bible declares:

And the dragon was wroth [enraged] with the woman, and went to make war with the remnant of her seed, which keep the

> commandments of God, and have the testimony of Jesus Christ ... the testimony of Jesus is the spirit of prophecy. Revelation 12:17; 19:10 (KJV)

Seventh-day Adventists believe that God has raised them up to fulfill this exact Scripture —to become "the remnant" church of Bible prophecy. By God's love and grace (not by works), we are committed to believing in Jesus Christ and keeping "the commandments of God," including the fourth about "the seventh-day" Sabbath (see Exod. 20:8–11).

The last part of Revelation 12:17 declares that God's commandment-keeping "remnant" will also "have the testimony of Jesus Christ" which is "the spirit of prophecy." Rev. 19:10. Adventists believe this applies to them, too, for in the early history of our movement God gave "the spirit of prophecy"—which included visions, dreams, and prophetic guidance—to a woman named Ellen G. White (1827-1915). Adventists don't believe Mrs. White's writings constitute another Bible, or replace the Bible, but rather that her ministry and Bible-based writings are simply part of the fulfillment of God's promise that in "the last days" He would give "visions," "dreams," and prophetic guidance to certain "sons" and "daughters" to help guide His church in harmony with His Word (see Acts 2:16–18).

Throughout this book, you will read quotes from the Bible and Mrs. White's writings—often referred to as "the spirit of prophecy." If you have never read these writings, get ready for a special blessing! Of course, every teaching and doctrine must be tested by a "Thus saith the Lord" (see Isa. 8:20; 1 Thess. 5:21).

Seventh-day Adventists also believe that, among all the various churches and denominations on earth today, their church alone has been divinely commissioned by God Himself—similar to His calling of ancient Israel—to preach the mighty Three Angels' Messages of Revelation 14:6–12 "to every nation, tribe, tongue, and people" (vs. 6) to prepare men, women, and children for the soon return of Jesus Christ (vs. 14–16). Because they keep "the seventh-day" Sabbath and believe in the soon return (Advent) of Jesus, they are called "Seventh-day Adventists." Search far and wide, and you won't find another fully-organized Christian denomination except the Seventh-day Adventist Church that is now preaching the Three Angels' Messages worldwide.

Ellen White wrote:

In a special sense Seventh-day Adventists have been set in the world as watchmen and light bearers. To them has been entrusted the last warning for a perishing world. On them is shining wonderful light from the word of God. They have been given a work of the most solemn import—the proclamation of the first, second, and third angels' messages. There is no other work of so great importance. They are to allow nothing else to absorb their attention.[1]

This God-ordained commission to Adventists to preach the Three Angels' Messages "to every nation" (Rev. 14:6) in these end-times parallels Jesus Christ's pre-ascension commission to His disciples to "Go therefore and make disciples of all the nations, baptizing them in the name of the Father and of the Son and of the Holy Spirit." Matt. 28:19

"Not if we can help it!" *snarls the devil to his angels.*

The following seven points should be soberly considered:

1. Satan and his angels *hate* the Holy Bible.

---

1. *Testimonies for the Church*, vol. 9, p. 19

2. They *hate* God's Remnant Church (Rev. 12:17).

3. They *hate* "the commandments of God" (Rev. 12:17;14:12).

4. They *hate* "the testimony of Jesus Christ" which is "the spirit of prophecy" (Rev. 12:17; 19:10).

5. They *hate* The Three Angels' Messages (Rev. 14:6–12).

6. They *hate* the commission to "Go … make disciples of all nations" (Matt. 28:19).

7. They *hate* the Father, the Son, and the Holy Spirit (Matt. 28:19).

Welcome to *Satan's War Against the Godhead.*

May God Himself richly enlighten those who read this book.

CHAPTER 1

IT IS WRITTEN

Words are important. Especially inspired words. When tempted by Satan, Jesus Christ firmly replied:

> *It is written,* "Man shall not live by bread alone, but by *every word* that proceeds from the mouth of God." Matthew 4:4 (emphasis added)

Thus "It is written" was our Savior's weapon in His deadly conflict with the fallen foe. And He didn't just rely on "It is written" in a general sense, but on "It is written" in a specific sense. When Satan attacked, Christ fought back by quoting *specific words from God.* To Jesus, man is not to live by a few words, or by many words, but by *"every word* that proceeds from the mouth of God." God's words should be our weapon, too, in our daily battle against the evil one.

Closely following Christ's example of relying on divinely inspired words rather than on mere human words, Paul wrote to the Corinthians:

> My speech and my preaching were not with *persuasive words of human wisdom,* but in demonstration of the Spirit and of power, that your faith should not be in the wisdom of men but in the power of God ... These things we also speak, *not in words which man's wisdom teaches but which the Holy Spirit teaches,* comparing spiritual things with spiritual.1 Corinthians 2:4, 5 (emphasis added)

Our ultimate reliance should be on *"words ... which the Holy Spirt teaches."* Personally, I believe that if each of us would humbly receive, wholly submit to, and consistently rely on what God says in *His inspired writings,* there would be far fewer controversies in His Church.

Paul also advised us to:

Avoid foolish and ignorant disputes, knowing that they generate strife. And a servant of the Lord must not quarrel but be gentle to all, able to teach, patient, in humility correcting those who are in opposition, if God perhaps will grant them repentance, so that they may know the truth, and that they may come to their senses and escape the snare of the devil, having been taken captive by him to do his will. 2 Timothy 2:23–26

Here we are urged to "avoid foolish and ignorant disputes" which "generate strife." God doesn't want to see constant disputing, bickering, fighting, backstabbing, and "strife" inside His Church, so we should "avoid" such things as much as possible. He also wants His servants to be "gentle to all," "patient," and to reveal deep "humility." If these virtues are absent from our characters, we might unconsciously drift into "the snare of the devil" and end up being "taken captive by him to do his will."

What a frightening thought.

"God is in heaven, and you on earth," wrote Solomon, "therefore let your words be few." Eccl. 5:2. This wise man also wrote that "a

fool's voice is known by his many words."
Vs. 3. Concerning the Deity, there are some
things we know, but much we don't know and
should remain silent about. "The secret things
belong to the LORD our God," wrote Moses,
"but those things which are revealed belong to
us and to our children forever." Deut. 29:29.
About the Eternal, we only know what He
tells us. Beyond that, we shouldn't speculate,
but should "be content" (Heb. 13:5) with
what God has revealed.

Notice these additional warnings about not
diverging from the Word of the Lord:

> Every word of God is pure;
> He is a shield to those who put
>   their trust in Him.
> Do not add to His words,
> Lest He rebuke you, and you
>   be found a liar.
> Proverbs 30:5, 6

For I testify to everyone who hears the
words of the prophecy of this book: If
anyone adds to these things, God will add
to him the plagues that are written in this
book; and if anyone takes away from the
words of the book of this prophecy, God

shall take away his part from the Book of Life, from the holy city, and from the things which are written in this book. Revelation 22:18, 19

Paul urged the Corinthians "not to think beyond what is written." 1 Cor. 4:6. This doesn't mean we should only use biblical words in all our conversations. After all, the words "Facebook" and "YouTube" aren't in the Bible, etc. etc. etc. But God's counsel does mean that when it comes to what we believe and teach about spiritual truths, we stick like glue to what He has inspired. The warning, "Do not add to His words," should be taken seriously.

Mrs. White wrote:

The revelation of Himself that God has given in His word is for our study. This we may seek to understand. But beyond this we are not to penetrate. The highest intellect may tax itself until it is wearied out in conjectures regarding the nature of God; but the effort will be fruitless. This problem has not been given us to solve. No human mind can comprehend God. Let not finite man attempt to interpret

Him. Let none indulge in speculation regarding His nature. Here silence is eloquence. The Omniscient One is above discussion.[1]

Concerning our conflict with evil, she also wrote:

Let Satan always be confounded by the words, "It is written."[2]

Confounding the devil is what this book aims to do.

---

1. *Testimonies for the Church*, vol. 8, p. 279
2. *Letters and Manuscripts*, vol. 20, Lt 188, 1905, par. 16

CHAPTER 2

THE GODHEAD

Paul wrote:

> For since the creation of the world His invisible attributes are clearly seen, being understood by the things that are made, even His eternal power and **Godhead**, so that they are without excuse. Romans 1:20 (emphasis added)

Here Paul points us back to "the creation of the world." While many details about The Eternal lie far beyond our feeble, human comprehension, some things may be "clearly seen," and even "understood,"—specifically, *"His eternal power and Godhead."* As you will soon discover, when we closely examine what Moses wrote about "the creation of the world," the forming of Adam and Eve, their fall, and the time when the tower of Babel was being built, we can learn much about what the "Godhead" is all about.

To the world-wise Athenians, Paul declared:

We ought not to think that **the Godhead** is like unto gold, or silver, or stone, graven by art and man's device. Acts 17:29 (KJV, emphasis added)

Paul also wrote:

Beware lest anyone cheat you through philosophy and empty deceit, according to the tradition of men, according to the basic principles of the world, and not according to Christ. For in Him dwells all the fullness of **the Godhead** bodily; and you are complete in Him, who is the head of all principality and power. Colossians 2:8–10 (emphasis added)

Here Paul warned us to "beware" of being seduced by human "philosophy," "empty deceit," "the tradition of men," and "the basic principles of the world" that deceptively veer away from our Lord Jesus "Christ" in whom

"dwells all the fullness of *the Godhead bodily.*"
You will learn more about "Christ" and "the Godhead" shortly.

In the Beginning

The Holy Bible begins with this sublime sentence: "In the beginning God created the heaven and the earth." Gen. 1:1. Although Moses didn't use the word "Godhead" when he wrote Genesis, he did write other things that help us begin to understand its meaning. Concerning what happened on the sixth day of Creation Week, Moses then wrote this monumental sentence:

Then God said, "Let *Us* make man in *Our* image, according to *Our* likeness." Genesis 1:26 (emphasis added)

Here a grand truth is revealed that can hardly be overemphasized. Let this sink in: In the first chapter of the Bible we see the words "God," "Us," and "Our" closely linked together. Ellen White commented insightfully:

After the earth was created, and the beasts upon it, the Father and Son carried out their purpose, which was designed before the fall of Satan, to make man in their own image. They had wrought together in the creation of the earth and every living thing upon it. And now God says to His Son, "Let us make man in our image."[1]

Thus "God" (the Father) said to His Son, "Let Us make man in Our image." A close look at these words reveal that humanity was made in the image of *both the Father and the Son.* The word "Our" also reveals Their deep unity in thought and action.

Where was the Holy Spirit? While we don't know the details, we do know that immediately after Moses wrote, "In the beginning God created the heaven and the earth," he also wrote: "And *the Spirit of God* was hovering over the face of the waters." Gen. 1:2 (emphasis added). Thus "the Spirit of God" (the Holy Spirit) was involved in Creation Week in some way, even though Genesis 1 doesn't provide any more specific information.

This close connection between "God" and "Us" appears again in Genesis 3. Shortly after Adam and Eve sinned, "Then the LORD God

---

1. *Spiritual Gifts,* vol. 3, p. 33

said, 'Behold, the man has become like one of Us, to know good and evil.' " Gen. 3:22. Similar words appear again a few chapters later. After men began building a tall tower to escape a future flood, "The LORD said … 'Come, let Us go down and there confuse their language … ' " Gen. 11:6, 7

Thus, *three times* at the beginning of the Bible—in Gen. 1:26; 3:22; 11:6, 7—we see a close connection between "God," "Lord God," "Lord," "Us," and "Our."

Genesis chapters 1 and 2 provide even more information that can help us better understand the concept of unity. Moses wrote: "So the evening and the morning were the first day." Gen. 1:5. The original Hebrew word he used now translated "first" in our English Bibles is "echad"—which is often used in Scripture to indicate unity. In Genesis 1:5, two separate parts ("the evening and the morning"), blended together, made up "the first ("echad") day."

Four verses later, we read:

Then God said, "Let the *waters* under the heavens be gathered together into *one* place, and let the dry land appear"; and it was so. Genesis 1:9 (emphasis added)

Here the word translated "one" is also "echad." Similar to verse 5 where two parts ("the evening and the morning") united made up "the first day," now plural "waters" were gathered together into "one place." The next time "echad" is used in Scripture is in Genesis 2:24. Notice closely:

Therefore a man shall leave his father and mother and be joined to his wife, and *they* shall become *one* [echad] *flesh.*" Genesis 2:2 (emphasis added)

In our normal vocabulary, sometimes the word "one" indicates one particular thing, like one hat, one dog, or one cat. The Bible often uses the word "one" in that way. But other times, "one" indicates a united one. In Genesis 2:24, the words, "one flesh," clearly mean *a united one.* After they were married, Adam and Eve did "become one flesh." They still remained two distinct persons, but they also became "one flesh" on their honeymoon, and beyond.

Thus, the evidence seems to suggest that, shortly after God said, "Let Us make man in Our image," that the Father and His Son created a man and a woman to somehow give us a window into Their own mysterious unity.

In a similar (although not exact) sense, Jesus prayed that His disciples might be "made perfect in one" (John 17:23) as He is one with His Father (see John 17:11). Writing about God's Church, Paul expressed a similar truth when he wrote that "the body [the church] is one, and has many members." 1 Cor. 12:12. Here again we see that the word "one" sometimes means more than one becoming united in one. Putting these pieces together we discover that just like there is a united "Us" in heaven, and in a similar way (though not exact) to how Adam and Eve became united in one, even so is it God's plan is that the members of "the body" (the church) also become united in "one"—just as Jesus is one with His Father.

Pretty deep thoughts, don't you think?

The next question is: Who specifically is "Us" referred to in Genesis 1:26; 3:22; and 11:6, 7? Based on Ellen White's previous comment about Genesis 1:26, we know "Us" refers to the Father and His Son, who are united in a deep bond of togetherness. Yet Mrs. White's inspired writings reveal more. Notice carefully:

The Godhead was stirred with pity for the race, and *the Father, the Son, and the Holy Spirit gave themselves* to the working out of the plan of redemption. In order fully to carry out this plan, it was decided that Christ, the only begotten Son of God, should give himself an offering for sin."[2]

These inspired words take us back to the time when Adam and Eve first committed sin, as described in Genesis 3. At that time— which wasn't long after God said, "Let Us make man in Our image,"—"The Godhead" was "stirred with pity" for our fallen race. In this inspired statement, we also see that "The Godhead" not only refers to the Father and His Son, but to "the Father, the Son, *and the Holy Spirit*" who unitedly *"gave themselves* to the working out of the plan of redemption."

Is it possible for tiny humans to fully comprehend such things? No, for even "The mightiest created intelligence cannot grasp divinity."[3] On the other hand, we can still grasp "those things which are *revealed*" which now "belong to us and to our children." Deut. 29:29

---

2. *Review and Herald,* May 2, 1912, par. 3 (emphasis added)
3. *Signs of the Times,* June 27, 1895

Here is another inspired paragraph that "belong[s] to us" and further clarifies the meaning of the term "Godhead":

[When Jesus walked on earth] The whole ocean of divine love was flowing forth from its great center. *The Godhead—the Father, the Son, and the Holy Spirit—were working in behalf of man.* Every power in the heavenly universe was put into activity to carry forward the plan of redemption."[4]

And another:

We are to cooperate with *the three highest powers in heaven,—the Father, the Son, and the Holy Ghost,—*and these powers will work through us, making us workers together with God.[5]

All of these inspired statements plainly reveal the deep unity between "the Father, the Son, *and* the Holy Ghost." We might call Them a Heavenly Family. In my own earthly

---

4. *Review and Herald,* Jan. 7, 1902 (emphasis added)
5. *Special Testimonies, Series B, No. 7,* p. 51

family, there are four of us: Me, my wife Kristin, our son Seth, and our daughter Abby. If some evil person were to attack my wife, or my children, let me assure you that such an attack would be on me, too.

In other words, if you attack my family, *you attack me.*

It's the same with "the Father, the Son, and the Holy Spirit." To wage war on any one of Them, is to wage war on the entire Heavenly Family. This illustrates how Satan and his rebel angels are now making war against the Godhead.

In Chapter 3, we'll look closer at the details.

CHAPTER 3

THE FATHER, THE SON, AND THE HOLY SPIRIT

The Father

In the book of John, we read:

Jesus spoke these words, lifted up His eyes to heaven, and said: "**Father**, the hour has come. Glorify Your Son, that Your Son also may glorify You, as You have given Him authority over all flesh, that He should give eternal life to as many as You have given Him. And this is eternal life, that they may know You, the only true God, and Jesus Christ whom You have sent." John 17:1–3 (emphasis added)

In the book of Matthew, we also read:

Jesus answered and said, "I thank You,

Father, Lord of heaven and earth, that You have hidden these things from the wise and prudent and have revealed them to babes. Even so, **Father**, for so it seemed good in Your sight. All things have been delivered to Me by **My Father**, and no one knows the Son except **the Father**. Nor does anyone know **the Father** except the Son, and the one to whom the Son wills to reveal Him." Matthew 11:25–27 (emphasis added)

In Matthew 11:25–27 we learn that:

1. The "Father" is "Lord of heaven and earth."

2. No one knows "the Father except the Son."

3. No one knows "the Son except the Father."

4. Only the Son can fully reveal the Father to us.

5. These things are "hidden from the wise and prudent."

6. But God has "revealed them to babes."

Points 5 and 6 teach the vital lesson that only those spiritually small and humble enough to receive God's revelation—above the words of proud, worldly-wise men—can understand the Father and His Son. This again repeats the message that in order to rightly understand God, we must rely on what He reveals about Himself—especially in His Word. The book *Steps to Christ* says:

Nature and revelation alike testify of God's love. **Our Father** in heaven *is the source of life, of wisdom, and of joy.*[1]

In Daniel 7:9, 10, the prophet beheld "the Ancient of days" take His seat when "the judgment was set and the books were opened." Ellen White commented:

Thus was presented to the prophet's vision the great and solemn day when the characters and the lives of men should pass in review before the Judge of all the earth, and to every man should be

---

1. *Steps to Christ*, p. 9 (emphasis added)

rendered "according to his works." The Ancient of days is **God the Father**. Says the psalmist, "Before the mountains were brought forth, or ever thou hadst formed the earth and the world, even from everlasting to everlasting, thou art God." [Psalm 90:2.] *It is He, the source of all being, and the fountain of all law,* that is to preside in the Judgment.[2]

Then "one like the Son of Man" came "to the Ancient of days" to represent God's people (verse 13). "The Son of Man" refers to Jesus Christ, our Savior.

Jesus Christ

The New Testament reveals that Jesus Christ is God's Son:

For God so loved the world that He gave **His only begotten Son**, that whoever believes in Him should not perish but have everlasting life. John 3:16 (emphasis added)

---

2. *The Great Controversy,* p. 479 (emphasis added)

These are written that you may believe that **Jesus is the Christ, the Son of God**, and that believing you may have life in His name. John 20:31 (emphasis added)

Whoever confesses that **Jesus is the Son of God**, God abides in him, and he in God. 1 John 4:15 (emphasis added)

But the Scripture says more. The New Testament also plainly states that Jesus Christ Himself is God, as it is written:

In the beginning was the Word, and the Word was with God, and **the Word was God** ... and the Word become flesh, and dwelt among us. John 1:1, 14 (emphasis added)

Ellen White commented:

Before men or angels were created, the Word was with God, and was God.[3]

Quoting John 1:3 which states, "All things were made through Him [Christ], and

---

3. *Review and Herald,* April 5, 1906

without Him [Christ] nothing was made that was made," Ellen White also wrote:

> If Christ made all things, He existed before all things. The words spoken in regard to this are so decisive that no one need be left in doubt. *Christ was God essentially, and in the highest sense. He was with God from all eternity, God over all, blessed forevermore.*[4]

The point is critical. The fact that Jesus is "the Son of God" does not make Him a lesser deity. Definitely not. "Christ was God *essentially,* and in *the highest sense.*" Turning to the book of Hebrews, we read:

> God, who at various times and in various ways spoke in time past to the fathers by the prophets, has in these last days spoken to us by **His Son**, whom He has appointed heir of all things, through whom also He made the worlds; who being the brightness of His glory and **the express image of His person**, and upholding all things by the word of His

---

4. *Ibid.,* (emphasis added)

power, when He had by Himself purged our sins, sat down at the right hand of the Majesty on high. Hebrews 1:1–3 (emphasis added)

Here we learn that Jesus is not only God's Son, but He is also the one "through whom He [the Father] made the worlds." Jesus is also "the express image of His [the Father's] person." In other words, when we see the Son, *we see an exact representation of His Father.* So much so, that Jesus even said, "He that has seen Me has seen the Father." John 14:9. Beyond this, Hebrews chapter 1 reveals an astonishing truth:

To *the Son, He* [the Father] *says: "Your throne, O God, is forever and ever;* a scepter of righteousness is the scepter of Your kingdom." Hebrews 1:8 (emphasis added)

Thus, the idea that the word "God" applies *exclusively* to the Father is contradicted by the Father Himself who in Hebrews 1:8 acknowledged His Son as "God." In Scripture, God *alone* should be worshiped. "Worship God" (Rev. 19:10), said a holy angel to John after he mistakenly bowed before him. The fact that in Hebrews 1, verse 6, the Father also said about

His Son, "Let all the angels of God worship Him," proves that both the Father and the Son are fully "God" and worthy of worship.

Ellen White explains their distinctiveness, and the exact nature of their deep unity:

> They are one in purpose, in mind, in character, but not in person. *It is thus that God and Christ are one.*[5]

Jesus told some Jews, "Before Abraham was, I AM." John 8:58. Ellen White commented:

> With solemn dignity Jesus answered, "Verily, verily, I say unto you, Before Abraham was, I AM." Silence fell upon the vast assembly. The name of God, given to Moses to express the idea of the eternal presence, had been claimed as His own by this Galilean Rabbi. *He had announced Himself to be the self-existent One,* He who had been promised to Israel, "whose goings forth have been from of old, from the days of eternity." Micah 5:2, margin.[6]

---

5. *Testimonies for the Church,* vol. 8, p. 269 (emphasis added)
6. *The Desire of Ages,* p. 469 (emphasis added)

Jesus declared, "I am the resurrection, and the life." In Christ is life, *original, unborrowed, underived.* "He that hath the Son hath life." The divinity of Christ is the believer's assurance of eternal life.[7]

Christ is the pre-existent, *self-existent Son of God* ... In speaking of His pre-existence, Christ carries the mind back through dateless ages. He assures us that *there never was a time when He was not in close fellowship with the eternal God.* He to whose voice the Jews were then listening had been with God as one brought up with Him.[8]

According to these inspired statements, "the self-existent Son of God" has existed "for dateless ages" and "there *never was a time*" when "He was not in close fellowship with the eternal God." Thus our Lord Jesus Christ *had no beginning.* So what does the Bible mean that Jesus was "begotten"? The last book of the Bible refers to Jesus as "the first begotten of the dead" (Rev. 1:5), which applies to His resurrection. The same application of

---

7. *Ibid.,* p. 530 (emphasis added)
8. *Signs of the Times,* August 29, 1900 (emphasis added)

"begotten" to Christ's resurrection can also been seen in Acts 13:33. Beyond what the Bible says, we don't know the fullness of what "begotten" means. But we can be certain that trying to fully comprehend "the Father" and His "only begotten Son" *based on human relationships has severe limitations.*

For instance, in normal human relationships, in order for a man to become a father he must have a physical union with a woman, and in order for a son to be born or begotten, he must have two parents—one male, and one female. As to the Godhead, there is no hint in Holy Scripture that such a thing has ever taken place. "You thought that I was altogether like you," God explained through David, "But I will rebuke you, and set them in order before your eyes." Psa. 50:21

The Godhead is *not* "altogether" like us.

Remember, "The secret things belong to the LORD our God." Deut. 29:29. It is God's divine prerogative to keep some things mysterious and "secret." But other things have been "revealed," such as "there never was a time" when Jesus "was not in close fellowship with the eternal God," that He is "God" (John 1:1), "the express image of His [Father's] person" (Heb. 1:3), the "Mighty God" and

"Everlasting Father" (Isa. 9:6), "the Almighty" (Rev. 1:8, 11), "the true God" (1 John 5:20), the great "I AM" (John 8:56), is "self-existent,"[9] and fully "equal with God." Phil. 2:6

Jesus often called Himself "the Son of Man" (Mark 9:31), which means He was truly a man. Similarly, when He spoke of God as His Father, and declared Himself "the Son of God" (John 10:36; Rev. 2:18), this means He is fully God. The Jews understood exactly what He meant, which is why they said, "For a good work we do not stone You, but for blasphemy, and *because You, being a Man, make Yourself God."* John 10:33 (emphasis added)

Our Lord and Savior Jesus Christ isn't a mini-God, lesser God, inferior God, or Father-derived-God. No, no, no. When Paul wrote that "in Him [Christ] dwells *all the fullness* of the Godhead bodily" (Col. 2:9), this means that Jesus isn't merely God-like, but God in His fullness. Indeed, Christ is God "in *the highest sense. He was with God from all eternity, God over all, blessed forevermore."*[10][11]

After His glorious resurrection—which

---

9. *The Desire of Ages,* p. 469

10. *Review and Herald,* April 5, 1906 (emphasis added)

11. For more information, read "Proof that Jesus Christ is Yahweh" by Rob Durkin at https://theheavenlytrio.com/yahweh

meant the ultimate defeat and doom of Satan and his vast army of confederate angels— Thomas confessed to His Savior, "My Lord and my God!" John 20:28. Jesus didn't rebuke His enlightened disciple for being in error. Instead:

> Jesus said to him, "Thomas, because you have seen Me, *you have believed.* Blessed are those who have not seen and *yet have believed."* John 20:29 (emphasis added)

The Holy Spirit

Concerning the Holy Spirit, Ellen White wrote:

> **The nature of the Holy Spirit is a mystery. Men cannot explain it, because the Lord has not revealed it to them.** Men having fanciful views may bring together passages of Scripture and put a human construction on them, but the acceptance of these views will not strengthen the church. **Regarding such mysteries, which are too deep for human understanding, silence is golden.**[12]

---

12. *Acts of the Apostles,* p. 52 (emphasis added)

Here we are told that:

1. "The nature of the Holy Spirit is a mystery."

2. We "cannot explain it" because "the Lord has not revealed it."

3. We should avoid "fanciful views" about the Holy Spirit.

4. We should also avoid bringing "together passages of Scripture" and putting "a human construction on them" in such a way that "will not strengthen the church." Thus *strengthening the church*, rather than dividing it, should be one of our top priorities (more on this later).

5. Because such mysteries "are too deep for human understanding, silence is golden."

Thus, concerning the exact nature of the Holy Spirit, we should often keep silent, rather than acting like a fool whose "voice is known by his many words." Eccl. 5:3

The Holy Bible calls the Holy Spirit "the

Spirit of God" (Gen. 1:2), "My Spirit" (Gen. 6:3), "the Spirit of life" (Rom. 8:2), "the Spirit of Christ" (Rom. 8:9), and "the Spirit of truth" sent to guide us into "all truth" (John 16:13) revealed in God's Word (John 17:17). The Holy Spirit convicts us of sin (John 16:8), reveals the things of Jesus Christ to us (John 16:14), has His own "mind" (Rom. 8:27), and sometimes speaks directly (Acts 13:2; Heb. 3:3–11; Rev. 14:13). He can be "grieved" (Eph. 4:30), and even blasphemed (Matt. 12:31).

Jesus said,

And I will pray the Father, and He will give you **another Helper**, that He may abide with you forever; even **the Spirit of truth**, whom the world cannot receive, because it neither sees **Him** nor knows **Him**; but you know **Him**, for **He** dwells with you and will be in you. I will not leave you orphans; I will come to you. John 14:16–18 (emphasis added)

If anyone loves Me, he will keep My word; and My Father will love him, and We will come to him and make Our home with him. John 14:23

However, when **He, the Spirit of truth**, has come, **He** will guide you into all truth; for **He** will not speak on **His own authority**, but whatever **He** hears **He** will speak; and **He** will tell you things to come. **He** will glorify Me, for **He** will take of what is Mine and declare it to you. John 16:13, 14 (emphasis added)

In these sacred verses, we learn that:

1. The Holy Spirit is *"another* Helper" separate from Christ.

2. The Holy Spirit is a "He."

3. The Father will send "Him" to us.

4. Through the Holy Spirit, *Jesus reveals Himself to us.*

5. The Holy Spirit doesn't "speak on His own authority." (The KJV says, "He shall not speak of himself.")

6. He speaks only what He hears from the Father and the Son.

7. He reveals the future to us based on God's Word.

8. He receives from Christ and shows His truths to us.

9. "He" (the Holy Spirit) will "glorify Me," said our Savior.

10. Through the Holy Spirit, both the Father and His Son will make Their home in our hearts.

In *The Desire of Ages,* pp. 669-672, Ellen White further explained what Jesus Christ taught about the Holy Spirit in John's gospel, chapters 14-16. There, she explained that "the Holy Spirit is Christ's representative" and "His successor on earth." Yet "the disciples still failed to understand Christ's words *in their spiritual sense.*" To make the truth clearer, Jesus "again explained His meaning. By the Spirit, He said, *He would manifest Himself to them.*"[13] Thus our Savior promised to *manifest Himself* through the Holy Spirit to His humble people.

---

13. *The Desire of Ages,* pp. 669,670 (emphasis added)

Ellen White wrote:

We want the Holy Spirit, which is Jesus Christ.[14]

She also wrote:

The Holy Spirit is the comforter, in Christ's name. *He personifies Christ, yet is a distinct personality.*[15]

How can the Holy Spirit "which is Jesus Christ," also have "a distinct personality" separate from Christ? We don't know, because His exact nature is beyond our finite comprehension. But we do know that the Holy Spirit is "Christ's representative," which means He represents Christ to us. We also know that both quotes above are true, just like a penny has a head side, and a tail side, yet both sides are part of the same coin. But again, "The nature of the Holy Spirit is a mystery. Men cannot explain it, because the Lord has not revealed it to them ... Regarding such mysteries, which are too deep for human

---

14. *Letters and Manuscripts,* vol. 9, Lt 66, 1894, par. 18
15. *Manuscript Releases,* vol. 20, p. 324 (emphasis added)

understanding, silence is golden."

John also wrote: "By this we know the Spirit of truth and the spirit of error." 1 John 4:6. The Holy Spirit is "the Spirit of truth," while "the spirit of error" is the spirit of Satan. The devil is "the spirit that now works in the children of disobedience." Eph. 2:2. Satan is also "a liar, and the father of it." John 8:44. Putting these Scriptures together, we conclude that Satan, the great deceiver and father of lies, is not only at war with "the Spirit of truth" (John 16:13), but with the entire Godhead.

Remember my family illustration.

When you attack one member of the Heavenly Family, you attack Them all.

To help us better understand this war, and the vital role of the Holy Spirit in helping us to be victorious over Satan, his evil angels, sin, and even our own fallen natures, God inspired Ellen White to pen these marvelous words:

In describing to His disciples the office work of the Holy Spirit, Jesus sought to inspire them with the joy and hope that inspired His own heart. He rejoiced because of the abundant help He had provided for His church. The Holy Spirit was the highest of all gifts that He could solicit from His

Father for the exaltation of His people. The Spirit was to be given as a regenerating agent, and without this the sacrifice of Christ would have been of no avail. The power of evil had been strengthening for centuries, and the submission of men to this satanic captivity was amazing. Sin could be resisted and overcome only through **the mighty agency of the Third Person of the Godhead**, who would come with no modified energy, but in the fullness of divine power. It is the Spirit that makes effectual what has been wrought out by the world's Redeemer. It is by the Spirit that the heart is made pure. Through the Spirit the believer becomes a partaker of the divine nature. Christ has given His Spirit as a divine power to overcome all hereditary and cultivated tendencies to evil, and to impress His own character upon His church.[16]

Here the battle lines are plainly drawn. On the one side is "Jesus," "His Father," and "the Holy Spirit;" while on the other side is "the power of evil" that has "been strengthening for centuries" and which is constantly seeking

16. *The Desire of Ages*, p. 671 (emphasis added)

to seduce humans into "satanic captivity."

How can we overcome Satan and his angels? There is only one way. "Sin could be resisted and overcome *only* through **the mighty agency of the Third Person of the Godhead**, who would come with no modified energy, but in the fullness of divine power." Think soberly with me. If the Holy Spirit is "the Third Person of the Godhead," there must be a Second Person of the Godhead, and a First Person of the Godhead.

Indeed. So there is.

There is "the Father," "the Son," and "the Holy Spirit." Matt. 28:19

"When He, the Spirit of truth is come, He will guide you into all truth." John 16:13

These sacred truths have been revealed in God's Word.

CHAPTER 4

"WAR BROKE OUT IN HEAVEN"

For thousands of years the human family has been in the midst of a titanic struggle between God and the devil. Lifting the veil, the book of Revelation informs us that this fierce conflict began in realms above:

> War broke out in heaven: Michael and his angels fought with the dragon; and the dragon and his angels fought, but they did not prevail, nor was a place found for them in heaven any longer. So the great dragon was cast out, that serpent of old, called the Devil and Satan, who deceives the whole world; he was cast to the earth, and his angels were cast out with him. Revelation 12:7–9

Our adversary is an incredibly intelligent, extraordinarily brilliant, mastermind of deception. In heaven, he deceived a third of God's holy angels, who are far smarter than we are. How could such a thing happen? What were the core issues?

The whole story has been "revealed" to us in Ellen White's masterful book, *Patriarchs and Prophets*. The first chapter, *Why Was Sin Permitted?*, begins with many Scriptures about the Father and His Son. The deep unity between them both is also clearly described:

"In the beginning was the Word, and the Word was with God, and the Word was God. The same was in the beginning with God." John 1:1, 2. Christ, the Word, the only begotten of God, was one with the eternal Father—one in nature, in character, in purpose—the only being that could enter into all the counsels and purposes of God.[1]

"The Father wrought by His Son in the creation of all heavenly beings."[2] (see John

1. *Patriarchs and Prophets,* p. 34
2. *Ibid.*

1:3; Eph. 3:9; Col. 1:16). Among the angels, one stood above them all: Lucifer, the light bearer. "Sin originated with him who, next to Christ, had been most honored of God and was highest in power and glory among the inhabitants of heaven."[3] At some point, the Father and His Son began planning the creation of the earth and human beings in Their own image. Because he was a created being—though highly exalted—Lucifer was not included in those planning sessions. Because "the Son of God was exalted above him, as one in power and authority with the Father," Lucifer somehow began to think new, strange, ominous thoughts. " 'Why?' questioned this mighty angel, 'should Christ have the supremacy? Why is He honored above Lucifer?"[4]

Here's where it all began.

Indulging a desire for self-exaltation, little by little, Lucifer became jealous of the Son of God. He then began to diffuse among the other angels his growing discontent at God's purposes, plans, government, and law. This mighty angel's particular discontent about the

3. *Ibid.*, p. 35
4. *Ibid.*, p. 37

status of God's Son above himself resulted in another meeting. Follow closely:

The King of the universe summoned the heavenly hosts before Him, that in their presence He might set forth *the true position of His Son* and show the relation He sustained to all created beings. *The Son of God shared the Father's throne, and the glory of the eternal, self-existent One encircled both.* About the throne gathered the holy angels, a vast, unnumbered throng—"ten thousand times ten thousand, and thousands of thousands" (Revelation 5:11.), the most exalted angels, as ministers and subjects, rejoicing in the light that fell upon them from the presence of the Deity. Before the assembled inhabitants of heaven the King declared that *none but Christ, the Only Begotten of God,* could fully enter into His purposes, and to Him it was committed to execute the mighty counsels of His will. The Son of God had wrought the Father's will in the creation of all the hosts of heaven; and *to Him, as well as to God, their homage and allegiance were due.* Christ was still to exercise divine power, in the creation of

the earth and its inhabitants. But in all
this He would not seek power or exaltation for Himself contrary to God's plan,
but would exalt the Father's glory and
execute His purposes of beneficence and
love.[5]

As I recently reread the first chapter of
Patriarchs and Prophets, it became crystal
clear to me that the root issue that ignited
the entire great controversy between Lucifer
and the King of the Universe boiled down to
the authority of God's Son and His relation-
ship to His Father. During a special meeting,
the Father clarified "the true position of His
Son." "The Son of God shared the Father's
throne, and the glory of the eternal, self-
existent One encircled both." The bright-
est angel in heaven couldn't stomach this.
Through his subtle deceptions, many "angels
in less exalted positions" had even concluded
that Lucifer himself "was the Ruler of heav-
en."[6] But he wasn't. God's Son was far above
Lucifer. "The exaltation of the Son of God *as
equal with the Father* was represented as an

---

5. *Ibid.,* p. 36 (emphasis added)
6. *This Day With God,* p. 256

injustice to Lucifer, who, it was claimed, was also entitled to reverence and honor."[7]

To dispute the supremacy of the Son of God, thus impeaching the wisdom and love of the Creator, had become the purpose of this prince of angels. To this object he was about to bend the energies of that master mind, which, next to Christ's, was first among the hosts of God.[8]

The Son of God was presented as being "equal with the Father." Eternally self-existent, He had no beginning. He shared His Father's throne. He was also Co-Creator in the formation of the angelic host, including Lucifer. But the highest angel rejected this deep revelation, and finally fought against it. "In great mercy, according to His divine character, God bore long with Lucifer."[9] Both the Father and His Son loved Their shiny created masterpiece. They pleaded with him, and so did many angels who remained loyal to Them both. Finally, this is what happened:

---

7. *Patriarchs and Prophets*, p. 37 (emphasis added)
8. *Ibid.*, p. 36 (emphasis added)
9. *Ibid.*, p. 39

[Lucifer] did not see whither he was drifting. But such efforts as infinite love and wisdom only could devise, were made to convince him of his error. His disaffection was proved to be without cause, and he was made to see what would be the result of persisting in revolt. Lucifer was convinced that he was in the wrong. He saw that "the Lord is righteous in all His ways, and holy in all His works" (Psalm 145:17); that the divine statutes are just, and that he ought to acknowledge them as such before all heaven. Had he done this, he might have saved himself and many angels. He had not at that time fully cast off his allegiance to God. Though he had left his position as covering cherub, yet if he had been willing to return to God, acknowledging the Creator's wisdom, and satisfied to fill the place appointed him in God's great plan, he would have been reinstated in his office. The time had come for a final decision; he must fully yield to the divine sovereignty or place himself in open rebellion. He nearly reached the decision to return, *but pride forbade him.* It was too great a sacrifice for one who had been so highly honored to confess that he had been in error, that his imaginings were false, and to yield to the authority which he had been working to prove unjust.[10]

"I will never again bow to God's Son!" declared Lucifer defiantly. Tragically, his own pride ruined him. "For himself, he was determined never again to acknowledge the authority of Christ. The only course remaining for him and his followers, he said, was to assert their liberty, and gain by force the rights which had not been willingly accorded them."[11] Finally, this mighty angelic prince took that fearful plunge. Deciding to boldly brave the consequences of his rebellion, Lucifer "fully committed himself to the great controversy *against his Maker.*"[12]

This is how Lucifer, the light bearer, became Satan, the devil, the great adversary of God and humanity.

Then "War broke out in heaven. Michael and his angels fought with the dragon; and the dragon and his angels fought, but they did not prevail, nor was a place found for them

---

10. *Ibid.* (emphasis added)
11. *Ibid.*, p. 40 (emphasis added)
12. *Ibid. (emphasis added)*

in heaven any longer. So the great dragon was cast out, that serpent of old, called the Devil and Satan, who deceives the whole world; he was cast to the earth, and his angels were cast out with him." Revelation 12:7–9

Today, the devil and his angels "deceive the whole world." In these last days, the conflict that began in heaven is nearing its close. Yet the core issues remain the same—and they concern the Father, His Son, and Their supreme, united authority.

"Why isn't the Holy Spirit mentioned in *Patriarchs and Prophets,* chapter 1?" some have asked. I can't give a definite answer, but perhaps the mystery lies in what Jesus said about the Holy Spirit: "He shall not speak of Himself." John 16:14. Apparently, the Holy Spirit doesn't sit upon a throne. He likes being in the background. But He has always existed as "the eternal Spirit" (Heb. 9:14), as you will discover in the next chapter.

CHAPTER 5

PIONEERS AND PANTHEISM

The Advent Movement was raised up to proclaim the Three Angels' Messages worldwide to prepare a people for the soon return of Jesus Christ (see Revelation 14:6–16). The movement is of God, yet its participants—though led by the Holy Spirit—are still weak, fallible mortals. Our early Adventist "pioneers" were just that, courageous *pioneers* who forged ahead. When we objectively examine Adventist history, we see that God led His people step by step. As He did, our pioneers sometimes adjusted their beliefs and practices.

"Happy is the man whom God corrects." Job 5:17

Our pioneers understood this practically.

As long-lost biblical truths became clearer, our pioneers abandoned many old ideas, and adopted new ones. They learned new things about the sanctuary (that it is in heaven—see Heb. 8:1, 2), the seventh-day Sabbath (that it isn't Sunday—see Ex. 20:8–11; Luke 23:54–56; 24:1), the vital importance of health principles (thus they should avoid pork, alcohol and tobacco—see Prov. 23:31–33; 1 Cor. 6:20, 10:31), the critical need for church organization (because God values order—see Matt. 16:18; Tit. 1:5), the unconscious state of the dead who await the resurrection (see Psa. 115:17; Eccl. 9:5; Dan. 12:2; 1 Cor. 15:51–54), and many other sacred truths.

In the 1880s and 1890s, as a result of the Holy Spirit working through anointed men like A.T. Jones and E.J. Waggoner,[1] Adventists also received more light about how "righteousness" can only come "by faith" in Christ alone (not by law-keeping—Rom. 3:19–28; 5:1; 9:31–33), that Jesus is "THE LORD OUR RIGHTEOUSNESS" (Jer. 23:5, 6), and that He is fully equal with the Father (Phil. 2:6)—for only thus could His mighty Sacrifice on Calvary legitimately atone for the world's sins of breaking God's law (see Rom. 3:21, 22; 1 Cor. 15:3; 1 John 2:2; 3:4). They

---

1. *Testimonies to Ministers,* pp. 91,92

also learned more about how fully receiving "THE LORD OUR RIGHTEOUSNESS" is the golden key to their being able to obey God's law of love by the power of the Holy Spirit (see Rom. 8:1, 4; Rev. 14:12).[2]

Their acceptance of these mighty biblical truths came about because our Adventist pioneers were humble enough, small enough, and teachable enough to let God Almighty correct and instruct them so they could follow His Word more perfectly.

Yet even more light was coming.

In 1894 the Lord's messenger wrote:

We must not for a moment think that there is no more light, no more truth to be given us. We are in danger of becoming careless, by our indifference losing the sanctifying power of truth, and composing ourselves with the thought, "I am rich and increased with goods, and have need of nothing." [Revelation 3:17.] While we must hold fast to the truths which we have already received, we must not look with suspicion upon any new light that God may send.[3]

---

2. See the author's book, *God's Last Message: Christ our Righteousness*

3. *Review and Herald,* Aug. 7, 1894

In the early 1900s, largely because some Adventists didn't fully accept the advanced messages of Jones and Waggoner about Jesus Christ and His Righteousness, a terrible crisis came to the Seventh-day Adventist Church about the nature and personality of God. Through the Holy Spirit, Ellen White saw it coming, and warned:

> Unless divine power is brought into the experience of the people of God, false theories and ideas will take minds captive, Christ and His righteousness will be dropped out of the experience of many, and their faith will be without power or life.[4]

At the heart of this new crisis was Dr. John Harvey Kellogg, the Medical Director of the Battle Creek Sanitarium, who in the early 1900s published his book entitled, *Living Temple.* "The publication of 'Living Temple' has brought about a crisis," Ellen White wrote.[5] That crisis, and God's solution to it, are clearly described in a small booklet

---

4. *Gospel Workers,* p. 161
5. *Special Testimonies,* Series B, Vol. 7, p. 48

entitled, *Testimonies for the Church Containing Letters to Physicians and Ministers Giving Messages of Warning and Words of Counsel and Admonition Regarding Our Present Situation.*

Adventists often call that little book, *Series B, Vol. 2 and 7.*

The core issue concerned subtle deceptions about "the presence and the personality of God." "The statements made in 'Living Temple' in regard to this point are not correct," the Lord's messenger warned.[6] In *Series B,* Kellogg's theories are referred to as "false ideas of God," "a wily tissue of lies," "schemes of satanic agencies," "insidious fallacies," "spiritualistic interpretations of the Scriptures," "charming philosophical speculations," and "hypnotism exercised by the father of lies." "Separate from the influence exerted by the book, *'Living Temple;'* " Ellen White urged Adventist physicians, ministers, and church members, "for it contains specious sentiments."[7]

About Kellogg, she wrote, "He has not heeded the testimonies that God through His Spirit has given. The books of the Bible

6. *Special Testimonies,* Series B, Vol. 2, p. 53
7. *Ibid.,* p. 49

containing most important instruction are disregarded because they say so much about a personal God. [Like Lucifer in heaven] He [Kellogg] has not known whither his feet were tending. But in his recent writings [*Living Temple*], his tendencies toward pantheism have been revealed."[8]

These statements pinpoint Kellogg's core deception: It was his stubborn, persistent disregard for "the testimonies that God through His Spirit has given," his rejection of plain Bible statements about "a personal God," and his dangerous "tendencies toward pantheism." "*Living Temple*" left "the impression that our God Omnipotent, who ruleth in the heavens and fills all the heavens, is to be found in flower, and leaf, and tree."[9] "Scientific, spiritualistic sentiments representing the Creator as an essence pervading all nature, have been given to our people ... "[10] "Pantheistic ideas regarding God in nature are framed by Lucifer, the fallen angel."[11]

Instead of philosophical, pseudo-scientific, speculative nonsense, God's people were urged

8. *Special Testimonies,* Series B, Vol. 7, p. 39

9. *Ibid.,* p. 50

10. *Ibid.,* p. 36

11. *Ibid.,* p. 49

"to have reverence for, and a knowledge of, a personal God"[12] as revealed in His Word. "Where is our security? How shall we guard against Satan's bewitching artifices?—By reading the Word of God with an intensity of desire to know Him in the light of revelation which He has left on record of Himself; by meditating on His precepts diligently. We are to obey His commands, *afraid to venture outside of divine revelation, and to indulge in fallacious reasoning.*"[13]

In a nutshell, Dr. Kellogg had strayed from "It is written."

Then—and I urge all readers of this book to follow closely—in the very next paragraph, the Lord's messenger explained exactly what "God" and "Us" want us to understand. Notice carefully:

> We are to cooperate with **the three highest powers in heaven—the Father, the Son, and the Holy Ghost**—and these powers will work through us, making us workers together with God.[14]

---

12. *Ibid.*, p. 50
13. *Ibid.*, pp. 50, 51 (emphasis added)
14. *Ibid.*, p. 51 (emphasis added)

If we are teachable enough to follow God's counsel and are "afraid to venture outside of divine revelation, and to indulge in fallacious reasoning," we will humbly receive this "testimony" from the Lord.

There are 64 pages in *Series B, Vol. 7.* On p. 62, near the end of the book, the writer again summarizes Kellogg's deceptions found in *Living Temple,* and God's solution to his delusions. As I quote from p. 62 below, notice carefully how Ellen White first explains Kellogg's deception about the "Godhead," and then the solution—which is *accepting the truth about the Father, the Son, and the Holy Spirit,* and fully submitting to Their guidance:

I am instructed to say, The sentiments of those who are searching for advanced scientific ideas are not to be trusted. Such representations as the following are made: "The Father is as the light invisible; the Son is as the light embodied; the Spirit is the light shed abroad." "The Father is like the dew, invisible vapor; the Son is like the dew gathered in beauteous form; the Spirit is like the dew fallen to the seat of life." Another representation: "The Father is like the invisible vapor; the Son is like the leaden cloud; the Spirit is rain fallen and working in refreshing power."

All these spiritualistic representations are simply nothingness. They are imperfect, untrue. They weaken and diminish the Majesty which no earthly likeness can be compared to. God cannot be compared with the things His hands have made. These are mere earthly things, suffering under the curse of God because of the sins of man. The Father cannot be described by the things of earth. **The Father is all the fulness of the Godhead bodily**, and is invisible to mortal sight.

The Son is all the fulness of the Godhead manifested. The Word of God declares Him to be "the express image of His person." "God so loved the world, that He gave His only begotten Son, that whosoever believeth in Him should not perish, but have everlasting life." Here is shown the personality of the Father.

The Comforter that Christ promised to send after He ascended to heaven, is **the Spirit in all the fulness of the Godhead,** making manifest the power of divine grace to all who receive and believe in Christ as a personal Saviour. **There are three living persons of the heavenly trio; in the name of these three great powers—the Father, the Son, and the Holy Spirit**—those who receive Christ by living faith are baptized, and these powers will co-operate with the obedient subjects of heaven in their efforts to live the new life in Christ …[15]

Here Ellen White provided a detailed explanation of "the Godhead." There are *"three* great powers" and *"three* living persons in the heavenly *trio,"* states the Spirit of Prophecy. These are inspired words, not mere human speculation. The words "three" and "trio" mean exactly that. They don't mean two, or just one. These "three" are *"three living persons."* Quoting Jesus Christ in Matthew 28:19, this statement also declares that **"in the name of these three great powers—the Father, the Son, and the Holy Spirit—those who receive Christ by living faith are baptized."**

---

15. *Ibid.,* p. 62 (emphasis added)

When our Adventist pioneers read such statements about "three living persons in the heavenly trio" and "these three great powers— the Father, the Son, and the Holy Spirit," many learned something new, and their Christian experience deepened, even beyond what they had formerly understood and experienced in their earlier years. They had previously received light about the Father.[16] During the Jones and Waggoner era they learned even more about His Son, His full equality with the Father, His mercy and love, His spotless righteousness, the magnitude of His Sacrifice, and about the power of His grace to enable them to obey God's law of love.[17] Then in the early 1900s, as the Kellogg crisis unfolded, they received even more information about the Godhead.

That's how the Heavenly Family works, step by step, as it is written: "The path of the just is like the shining sun, that shines ever brighter unto the perfect day." Prov. 4:18

16. See "A Declaration of the Fundamental Principles Taught and Practiced by the Seventh-day Adventists," Principle 1, published in 1872 & 1889

17. See the author's book, *God's Last Message: Christ our Righteousness*

CHAPTER 6

ALPHA, OMEGA, "MEET IT!"

The messages in *Series B* about "a personal
God," *"three* living persons," "the heavenly
trio," and "these *three* great powers—the
Father, the Son, and the Holy Spirit," are
unmistakably clear. Its plain warnings about
humbly submitting to "divine revelation" and
avoiding "false ideas of God," "a wily tissue of
lies," "schemes of satanic agencies," "insidious fallacies," "spiritualistic interpretations of
the Scriptures," and "charming philosophical
speculations," are also unmistakably clear.

Writing specifically about the spiritual
dangers affecting many Adventist physicians,
ministers, and church members through the
influence of *Living Temple,* the Lord's messenger wrote:

Be not deceived; many will depart from the faith, giving heed to seducing spirits and doctrines of devils. We have now before us **the alpha** of this danger. **The omega** will be of a most startling nature.[1]

It is obvious that "the alpha" concerned the many seductive teachings found within Dr. Kellogg's book. What about "the omega"? In recent years, many have speculated about its meaning. "Could this be the omega?" some suggest. "Or that?" As I have read and reread *Series B,* the true meaning of "the omega" seems much simpler.

Follow closely.

The statement above reads: "We have now [during the time of Dr. Kellogg] before us **the alpha** of *this danger.* **The omega** will be of a most startling nature." Thus "the alpha" is "the alpha of *this danger*"—which was Kellogg's pantheism. Again she wrote: "*Living Temple* contains **the alpha** of these theories. **The omega** *would follow in a little while.* I trembled for our people."[2] Thus, after "the alpha" delusion, "the omega would follow in

---

1. *Special Testimonies,* Series B, Vol. 2, p. 16 (emphasis added)
2. *Ibid.,* p. 53 (emphasis added)

a little while." Again, she wrote:

> Now the publication of "Living Temple" has brought about a crisis. *If the ideas presented in this book were received,* they would lead to the uprooting of the whole construction of the faith that makes Seventh-day Adventists a chosen, denominated people.[3]

Here Ellen White warned what would be *the results* (the omega) "IF the ideas presented in this book [*Living Temple,* the alpha] were received." Thus it seems to me that "the omega" would be *the results* that would follow inside God's Church IF "the alpha" (pantheism) was fully received. What results? It "would lead to the uprooting of the whole construction of the faith that makes Seventh-day Adventists a chosen, denominated people."

This would mean total disaster!

Writing specifically of what would result IF Kellogg's "false ideas of God" and his seductive "tendencies toward pantheism" were received, Ellen White wrote:

---

3. *Special Testimonies,* Series B, Vol. 7, pp. 48,49 (emphasis added)

The enemy of souls has sought to bring in the supposition that a great reformation was to take place among Seventh-day Adventists, and that this reformation would consist in giving up the doctrines which stand as the pillars of our faith, and engaging in a process of reorganization. Were this reformation to take place, what would result?—The principles of truth that God in His wisdom has given to the remnant church would be discarded. Our religion would be changed. The fundamental principles that have sustained the work for the last fifty years would be accounted as error. A new organization would be established. Books of a new order would be written. A system of intellectual philosophy would be introduced. The founders of this system would go into the cities and do a wonderful work. The Sabbath, of course, would be lightly regarded, as also the God who created it. Nothing would be allowed to stand in the way of the new movement. The leaders would teach that virtue is better than vice, but God being removed, they would place their dependence on human power, which, without God, is worthless. Their foundation would be built on the sand, and storm and tempest would sweep away the structure.[4]

This ominous paragraph has been speculatively applied to many deceptions under the sun. To me, first, we should exercise caution. Next, we should recognize and appreciate the specific context of her warning. Again, its *immediate context is pantheism* (the alpha), and to me, the paragraph above simply shows what would be the result (the omega) IF such ideas were fully received by God's Seventh-day Adventist Remnant Church of Bible Prophecy. Did that happen? Many today speculate about the answer, yet the Spirit of Prophecy actually answers this question in clear, simple, plain language. Mrs. White wrote:

One night a scene was clearly presented before me. A vessel was upon the waters, in a heavy fog. Suddenly the lookout cried, "Iceberg just ahead!" There, towering high above the ship, was a gigantic iceberg. An authoritative voice cried out, "Meet it!" There was not a moment's

---

4. *Ibid.*, pp. 39,40

hesitation. It was a time for instant action. The engineer put on full steam, and the man at the wheel steered the ship straight into the iceberg. With a crash she struck the ice. There was a fearful shock, and *the iceberg broke into many pieces,* falling with a noise like thunder upon the deck. The passengers were violently shaken by the force of the collision, but no lives were lost. *The vessel was injured, but not beyond repair.* She rebounded from the contact, trembling from stem to stern, like a living creature. *Then she moved forward on her way.*

Well I knew the meaning of this representation. I had my orders. I had heard the words, like a living voice from our Captain, "Meet it!" I knew what my duty was and that there was not a moment to lose. The time for decided action had come. I must without delay obey the command, "Meet it!"

That night I was up at one o'clock, writing as fast as my hand could pass over the paper. For the next few days I worked early and late, preparing for our people the instruction given me regarding the errors that were coming in among us.[5]

This ship-hitting-an-iceberg illustration reveals seven facts:

1. In the early 1900s, a terrible crisis came to the Advent people.

2. God's Church was like a ship sailing into "a gigantic iceberg."

3. "Meet it!" was the Lord's firm command to His people.

4. God's Church did "Meet it!" when His ship hit the ice.

5. "The iceberg broke into many pieces."

6. The ship (God's Church) "was injured, but not beyond repair."

7. After the crash, "*the ship moved forward on her way.*"

---

5. *Special Testimonies,* Series B, Vol. 2, pp. 55,56 (emphasis added)

Thus inspiration informs us that God's Seventh-day Adventist Remnant Church of Bible Prophecy met this crisis, passed through it, and then "moved forward on her way." In other words, "the alpha" (pantheism) was shattered "into many pieces," and *no catastrophic omega* followed "in a little while." Instead, God's Remnant Church, because it was supernaturally guided by "the Father, the Son, and the Holy Spirit" continued "forward on her way." From that time until today—in spite of its problems, challenges, some new alphas (errors), and some new omegas (the result of receiving new alphas)—God's organized Seventh-day Adventist Remnant Church has been steadily sailing forward and onward, preaching, baptizing, and spreading the Three Angels' Messages worldwide.

"His Truth is marching on."

Alleluia!

CHAPTER 7

THE WITNESS OF
1 JOHN 5:7

Here is 1 John 5:7 in the KJV and NKJV:

For there are three that bear record in
heaven, the Father, the Word, and the
Holy Ghost: and these three are one.
1 John 5:7 (KJV)

For there are three that bear witness in
heaven: the Father, the Word, and the
Holy Spirit; and these three are one.
1 John 5:7 (NKJV)

Both versions are nearly identical. Here is
1 John 5:7 in four other translations:

For there are three that testify. 1 John 5:7
(NIV)

So we have these three witnesses. 1 John 5:7 (NLT)

For there are three that testify. 1 John 5:7 (NET)

And the Spirit is the witness, because the Spirit is the truth. 1 John 5:7 (RSV)

As you can see, the NIV, NLT, NET, and RSV completely emasculate what is written in the KJV and NKJV translations of 1 John 5:7. The KJV and NKJV refer to "three" that bear record in heaven—"the Father," "the Word" [Jesus], and "the Holy Spirit." Yet the other versions listed are much different and *completely remove the Godhead.*

Many other translations do the same thing. What's up with this?

If you search online and read articles written by various theologians and scholars, you will discover that the reason the words about the Godhead in 1 John 5:7 are often left out of modern Bible translations is because these learned men have concluded that the complete verse (as found in the KJV and NKJV) "was not found in the earliest manuscripts," or "is not in any Greek manuscript before the 1600s."

Other arguments are given, too.

But, as they say, "There are two sides to every coin." Personally, I have read both sides of this issue. From the research that I have done, and from the books and articles I have read,[1] here are some problems with "The 1 John 5:7 Was Added Later Theory":

1. The translators of the King James Version, which now contains the full version of 1 John 5:7, had access to many ancient manuscripts written hundreds of years before their translation into English.

2. Numerous "early church fathers" quoted 1 John 5:7.

3. The complete 1 John 5:7 text was in the old Waldensian Bibles (old Latin) and in their confessions, which became the basis of the Olivetan Bible (French), which became the basis of the Geneva Bible (English) which became a foundation and forerunner of the King James Bible, and the later New King James Bible.

---

1. For example, see https://tinyurl.com/1john57belongs

4. Questioning the validity of 1 John 5:7 questions God's ability to watch over and preserve the accuracy of His Word (see Jer. 1:12; 2 Peter 1:19–21; 2 Tim. 3:16).

5. Questioning the validity of 1 John 5:7 introduces doubt as to what is inspired and what isn't inspired in God's Holy Word.

6. Questioning the validity of 1 John 5:7 also places the issue of deciding what is inspired and what isn't into the hands of theologians, translators, and scholars (which is a Catholic principle), *rather than letting God's Word itself be the standard by which we test all human theories* (a Protestant principle).[2]

Ellen White wrote:

But God will have a people upon the earth to maintain the Bible, and the Bible only, as the standard of all doctrines, and

---

2. For a fuller treatment of this topic, see *Answers to Objections to Our Authorized Bible,* by Benjamin Wilkinson, p. 77

the basis of all reforms. *The opinions of learned men,* the deductions of science, the creeds or decisions of ecclesiastical councils, as numerous and discordant as are the churches which they represent, the voice of the majority,—not one or all of these should be regarded as evidence for or against any point of religious faith. *Before accepting any doctrine or precept, we should demand a plain "Thus saith the Lord" in its support.*[3]

This inspired quote tells us to judge all human opinions and theories by God's Word, rather than judging God's Word by human opinions and theories. "The opinions of learned men"—as valuable as they sometimes are—are not the ultimate standard for what Christians should believe and teach. Another inspired quote tells us that:

The Waldenses were among the first of the peoples of Europe to obtain a translation of the Holy Scriptures. *Hundreds of years before the Reformation they possessed the Bible in manuscript in their native*

---

3. *The Great Controversy,* p. 595 (emphasis added)

tongue. They had the truth unadulterated, and this rendered them the special objects of hatred and persecution.[4]

Those old Waldensian Bibles *contained the full version of 1 John 5:7.* Because they stood strong on God's Word, these faithful followers of Jesus Christ were hated, persecuted, and cruelly butchered by Roman legions.[5]

In 1884, a series of unfortunate articles appeared in a prominent Adventist journal, *The Review and Herald,* in which the writer advocated "Differences in Degrees" of inspiration. Those articles created doubt and had a negative influence on Adventist members in Battle Creek, Michigan, and on students attending the Adventist Battle Creek College. A few years later, the Lord led Ellen White to counteract the woeful influence of those articles by writing:

Both in the [Battle Creek] Tabernacle and in the [Battle Creek] college the subject of inspiration has been taught, and finite men have taken it upon themselves to

---

4. *Ibid.,* p. 65 (emphasis added)
5. *Ibid.,* chapter 4

say that some things in the Scriptures were inspired and some were not. I was shown that the Lord did not inspire the articles on inspiration published in the Review [6], neither did He approve their endorsement before our youth in the college. When men venture to criticize the Word of God, they venture on sacred, holy ground, and had better fear and tremble and hide their wisdom as foolishness. God sets no man to pronounce judgment on His Word, selecting some things as inspired and discrediting others as uninspired. The testimonies have been treated in the same way; but God is not in this.[7]

From this inspired paragraph we learn that:

1. Those who criticize God's Word are on dangerous ground.

2. Instead, they should fear and tremble before the Lord, and "hide their wisdom as foolishness."

6. *Review and Herald,* January 15, 1884
7. *Selected Messages,* vol. 1, p. 23

3. It is not our work "to pronounce judgment upon His Word, selecting some things as inspired and discrediting others as uninspired."

4. The "testimonies have been treated in the same way; *but God is not in this.*"

We already read about how, during the Kellogg crisis, the Spirit of Prophecy through various testimonies clarified that "There are three living persons of the heavenly trio…—the Father, the Son, and the Holy Spirit …" and that "in the name of these three great powers—the Father, the Son, and the Holy Spirit—those who receive Christ by living faith are baptized." That latter quote repeats the words of our Lord Jesus Christ Himself when He commissioned His disciples to "Go therefore and make disciples of all the nations, baptizing them in the name of the Father and of the Son and of the Holy Spirit." Matt. 28:19

Following inspired counsels found in both the Bible (first) and the Spirit of Prophecy (next), let's look again at 1 John 5:7:

For there are three that bear witness in heaven: the Father, the Word, and the

Holy Spirit; and these three are one.
1 John 5:7 (NKJV)

Thus, there are "three" in heaven, "and these three are one." Biblically speaking, this verse applies to the Godhead, in which "these three are one." Thus 1 John 5:7 is another testimony about how "the Father, the Son, and the Holy Spirit" *are united as one Heavenly Team* in their loving efforts to save our souls.

1 John 5:7 is the Word of the Lord.

Some time ago, I was reflecting on how I too have in the past avoided using 1 John 5:7 because of doubts cast on that verse by various theologians. Then it struck me that by instilling into my mind such doubts, Satan had craftily removed from my own spiritual arsenal one of God's Scriptural weapons. *Not anymore,* I firmly decided, for I need every weapon I can wield in this fierce battle with our ancient foe.

In the same book of 1 John, the inspired apostle also wrote:

I have written to you, young men,
Because you are strong, *and the word of
   God abides in you,*

And you have overcome the wicked one.
1 John 2:14 (emphasis added)

It is "the wicked one" (and his army of evil angels) who are at war, not only with God's Word, but with the Godhead made up of "the Father, the Son, and the Holy Spirit." Ever since Lucifer and his angels first rebelled in heaven because they refused to accept the supreme status of God's Son, this war has been raging.

And remember, when Satan attacks God's Son, he makes war on the entire Heavenly Trio, because "these three are one." 1 John 5:7

The war continues to this day.

CHAPTER 8

THREE *UNITED* ANGELS WORLDWIDE

Carrying us down to earth's Final Days, the Bible predicts:

> The dragon was wroth [enraged] with the woman and went to make war with the remnant of her seed, which keep the commandments of **God**, and have the testimony of **Jesus Christ** ... [which is] **the spirit of prophecy**." Revelation 12:17; 19:10 (KJV, emphasis added)

This verse reveals an intense battle between the forces of good and evil. On the one side is "The dragon," representing Satan; while on the other side is "the remnant," which represents the Lord's chosen, end-time people. The Heavenly Trio are embedded in these verses, too: "God," "Jesus Christ," and "the spirit of prophecy"—which points to the Holy Spirit giving direct guidance to "the remnant" through the agency of the ministry and writings of Ellen White.

Therefore, firmly nestled inside these mighty, end-time verses, we discover *the Godhead* revealed: the Father, the Son, and the Holy Spirit. "The dragon" (Satan) "went to make war" with "the remnant" (God's end-time church) *and* the Heavenly Trio that is faithfully leading God's people.

While God's Remnant Church is described in Revelation 12:17, its distinct message is highlighted in Revelation 14:6–12 containing the first, second, and third angels' messages. Angel Three concludes with:

> Here is the patience of the saints; here are those who keep the commandments of **God** and the faith of **Jesus**. Revelation 14:12 (emphasis added)

The next verse says:

> Then I heard a voice from heaven saying to me, "Write: 'Blessed are the dead who die in the Lord from now on.' 'Yes,' **says**

the Spirit, 'that they may rest from their labors, and their works follow them.' "
Revelation 14:13 (emphasis added)

Did you catch that? Similar to Revelation 12:17 and 19:10, Revelation 14:12 and 13 also reveals the three mighty members of the Godhead: "God" (the Father), "Jesus" (the Son), and "the Spirit" (the Third Person of the Godhead). In vs. 13, the Holy Spirit speaks directly about faithful souls who have died during the time of the proclamation of the Three Angels' messages. *"Yes,"* says the Spirit, "that they may rest from their labors, and their works follow them." Rev. 14:13 (emphasis added). Surely this special blessing also rests on those godly but now-deceased Adventist pioneers who gave their all for Jesus Christ and His holy cause.

Consider this: The Seventh-day Adventist Church is a Heavenly Trio-led, organized body of believers raised up to communicate world-wide a trio of messages (the Three Angels) to counteract a counterfeit trio made up of "the dragon ... the beast ... [and] the false prophet." Rev. 16:13. Throughout history, Satan has always worked to counterfeit the genuine, and he is doing the same thing today through this counterfeit earthly trio. The battle is on. The stakes are high. It's life or death. This is why the devil is working so hard today to counterfeit the Godhead and sink the Adventist Church.

In *Series B,* Mrs. White warned that if Dr. Kellogg's devil-inspired pantheistic doctrines (the alpha) were fully received by God's "remnant" people, it "would lead to the uprooting of the whole construction of the faith that makes *Seventh-day Adventists a chosen, denominated people.*"[1] That's exactly what Lucifer wants. Thankfully, that fearful warning didn't materialize because God's Remnant "ship"—instructed by the Heavenly Trio working through Spirit of Prophecy—struck "the iceberg" head on and shattered it.

Then "the ship moved forward on her way."

Unfortunately, *Satan's War Against the Godhead* and against God's Seventh-day Adventist Remnant Church of Bible Prophecy didn't cease in the early 1900s. Hardly. Since then, in scattered places, some new alphas have appeared, with some new omegas (their consequences) following.

The battle keeps raging—even to this day.

---

1. *Special Testimonies,* Series B, Vol. 7, p. 48 (emphasis added)

Four Teachings Distracting
Adventists from their Mission

As I observe what is currently happening among Seventh-day Adventists, I have concluded that, unfortunately, there are four distinct teachings that (in many places) are dividing and distracting God's people. I also believe that, just as "the ship moved forward on her way" after the Kellogg crisis, it is also time for the members of God's Remnant Church to "move forward" and focus on our Godhead-ordained mission of giving the Three Angels' Messages worldwide.

Before listing these four teachings, I also want to publicly state my conviction that most of those who hold these beliefs are sincere. They want to discover inspired truth and follow it. Some are my friends. The last thing they want to do is hurt God's cause. Nevertheless, as the saying goes, "The devil is in the details." Similarly, I'm convinced that Satan and his dark army are now working behind the scenes through these four teachings to divide, distract, and confuse Adventists—just as they worked ingeniously during the Kellogg crisis.

Teaching 1:
The Father *Alone* is The One True God

Many who believe this consider themselves to be part of the "One True God" (OTG) movement. One key Bible verse used to support this teaching is John 17:3, where Jesus called His Father "the only true God." One OTG website I saw promoting this teaching showed a graphic of John 17:3 with the word "GOD" appearing in large letters, but the words "Jesus Christ" appeared in much smaller letters.

This illustrates my concern.

In a nutshell, my concern is: Father Up, Jesus Down.

Notice carefully that in John 17:3 Jesus stated that "eternal life" is to know the Father as "the only true God, AND Jesus Christ whom You have sent." Thus "eternal life" comes by knowing *both* the Father and His Son. In 1 John 1:1, 2, John specifically refers to Jesus as *"the Word* of life" and *"that eternal life* [Jesus] which was *with the Father,* and was manifested to us" (emphasis added). At the close of this same letter, John concluded:

And we know that *the Son of God* has come and has given us an understanding,

that we may know *Him* [the Son of God]
who is true; and we are in Him [the Son
of God] who is true, in *His* [the Father's]
*Son Jesus Christ. This is the true God and
eternal life.* 1 John 5:20 (emphasis added)

By closely comparing 1 John 1:1, 2 with
1 John 5:20, it seems to me (and to many
others[2]) that the key words, "the true God
and eternal life" equally apply to Jesus. Why
wouldn't they? Jesus is "true" (John 1:9; 6:32;
15:1), and He is "God." John 1:1. Just to
clarify, the words "the only true God" and
"one God" often *do* apply to the Father (see
1 Cor. 8:6; Eph. 4:6, 1 Tim. 2:5; Heb. 1:1;
Rev. 1:1, etc.); but as we have already seen
from many other Bible verses, similar words
equally apply to His Son. Jesus is also God
(see John 1:1; John 20:28; Heb. 1:8, 1 Tim.
3:16) and "the express image of His [the
Father's] person." Heb. 1:3. Ellen White also
describes a scene where a formerly lost person
approached a missionary in heaven and said,
"I was a heathen in heathen lands. You left
your friends and comfortable home and came
to teach me *how to find Jesus and believe in*

---

2. See https://theheavenlytrio.com/1john520

Him as the only true God."[3]

Thus, Jesus Christ is also "the only true God." He must be. For if He isn't, how can He *fully* reveal His Father? But He does reveal His Father perfectly, because when we see the Son, we see the Father (see John 14:9), they are "one" (see John 10:30), and within the Son is *"the fullness* of the Godhead bodily." Col. 2:9 (emphasis added)

In heaven, after the Father explained to the angels that His Son was equal with Himself, Lucifer protested. "No!" he stubbornly replied. In fact, *Patriarchs and Prophets,* chapter 1, reveals that it was this mighty angel's proud refusal to submit to the Father's clarification of the full Godhood status of His Son, and his sinful desire to exalt himself above God's Son, *that first ignited the entire great controversy.*

That's what turned Lucifer into the devil.

As I see it, any view that demotes Jesus is *dangerous.*

Teaching 2:
Jesus Christ Had a Beginning

Because Jesus as the "only *begotten* Son of

---

3. *Review and Herald,* Jan. 5, 1905 (emphasis added)

God," it is assumed by many in the OTG movement that Jesus *must have had a beginning*. Christ's being "begotten" is also often used as an argument that Jesus cannot have full and equal Godhood status with His Father. Various opinions are then offered as to what "begotten" means, such as birthed, generated, or emerged. But the end result is that "begotten" is interpreted to mean—based on a mere human understanding of earthly fathers giving birth to their sons—that our supreme *Lord and Savior Jesus Christ also had a beginning at some point in eons past.*

Similar to Teaching 1, the net result is: Father Up, Jesus Down.

Some of our Adventist pioneers also believed Jesus had a beginning, but the Spirit of Prophecy later corrected them.[4][5] Jesus is our great High Priest "after the order of Melchizedek." Psa. 110:4. In Genesis 14:18–20, Melchizedek appears in Scripture without a genealogy. Paul then wrote that Melchizedek (because he had no biblical genealogy) is "without father, without mother, without genealogy, *having neither beginning of days nor*

4. *The Desire of Ages,* p. 469
5. *Signs of the Times,* August 29, 1900 (emphasis added)

end of life, but made like the Son of God." Heb. 7:3 (emphasis added)

Christ *did* have an earthly genealogy (see Matt. 1), thus Heb. 7:3 must be indicating that *Christ had no beginning in eternity.* Again, Ellen White clarified this truth when she wrote: "Christ is the pre-existent, *self-existent Son of God* ... In speaking of His pre-existence, Christ carries the mind back through dateless ages. He assures us that *there never was a time when He was not in close fellowship with the eternal God.* He to whose voice the Jews were then listening had been with God as one brought up with Him."[6]

These statements are clear, and we should believe them. We have also been warned that "The very last deception of Satan will be to make of none effect the testimony of the Spirit of God."[7]

Teaching 3:
The Holy Spirit isn't a Person

Because the Holy Spirit is "the Spirit *of God*" and "the Spirit *of Christ,*" many in the OTG movement assume He isn't a separate Person. Yet

---

6. *Ibid.* (emphasis added)
7. *Letters and Manuscripts,* vol. 6, Letter 12, 1890

in Scripture, the Holy Spirit speaks as a Person. In Acts, *"The Holy Spirit said,* 'Now separate to *Me* Barnabas and Saul for the work to which *I* have called them.' " Acts 13:2 (emphasis added). Again, our Adventist pioneers weren't clear about this until the Spirit of Prophecy later enlightened them. Ellen White clarified: "The Holy Spirit is the comforter, in Christ's name. He personifies Christ, *yet is a distinct personality.*[8]

As the Kellogg crisis grew, she also wrote:

The Father, the Son, and the Holy Ghost, *powers infinite and omniscient,* receive those who truly enter into covenant relation with God.[9]

Thus, all three members of the mighty Godhead, including the Holy Spirit, are "infinite and omniscient." "Omniscient" means, "knowing everything." They also *each "receive* those who truly enter into covenant relation with God." And again, inspiration plainly identifies the Holy Spirit as "the Third *Person* of the Godhead."[10]

---

8. *Manuscript Releases,* vol. 20, p. 324 (emphasis added)

9. *Letters and Manuscripts,* vol. 15, Manuscript 27a, 1900 (emphasis added)

10. *The Desire of Ages,* p. 671 (emphasis added)

Here is a short summary of the teachings listed above:

1. The Father *alone* is "the only true God." This demotes Jesus.

2. Because Jesus is the "only *begotten* Son of God," He must have had a beginning. This also demotes Jesus.

3. Because the Holy Spirit is "the Spirit *of God*" and "the Spirit *of Christ,*" He can't be a separate Person.

Because the Adventist Church today doesn't officially accept Teachings 1-3, this sometimes leads to a fourth teaching:

Teaching 4:
The Organized Seventh-day Adventist Church is *No Longer* God's Remnant Church of Bible Prophecy

"Time to abandon ship!" some conclude, so they leave the organized Adventist church entirely. Worse still, many embark on a fearful mission to draw others away from the church. What about this?

The New Testament is clear that God's plan for His Church is that it be organized. "For this reason I left you in Crete," Paul told Timothy, "that you should *set in order* the things that are lacking, and appoint elders in every city as I commanded you." Titus 1:5 (emphasis added). The gifts of the Holy Spirit not only include apostles, prophets, pastors and teachers, but also "governments." 1 Cor. 12:28. "Let all things be done decently and in order" (1 Cor. 14:40), wrote Paul.

Just as the human body would be unable to function without cooperation between the brain, liver, heart, and lungs, even so the body of Christ (His Church) can't function healthfully without organization and order. "Christ designs that heaven's order, heaven's plan of government, heaven's divine harmony, shall be represented in His church on earth."[11]

In 1909—after pantheism was shattered—Ellen White penned a testimony entitled "The Spirit of Independence" to the delegates of the General Conference of Seventh-day Adventists gathered in Washington, DC.

By this time, Dr. Kellogg had left the Adventist Church entirely, and our church

11. *The Desire of Ages*, p. 680

headquarters was no longer in Battle Creek, Michigan.

Read her words carefully:

Oh, how Satan would rejoice if he could succeed in his efforts to get in among this people and disorganize the work at a time when thorough organization is essential and will be the greatest power to keep out spurious uprisings and to refute claims not endorsed by the word of God! *We want to hold the lines evenly, that there shall be no breaking down of the system of organization and order that has been built up by wise, careful labor. License must not be given to disorderly elements that desire to control the work at this time.*

Some have advanced the thought that, as we near the close of time, every child of God will act independently of any religious organization. But I have been instructed by the Lord that in this work there is no such thing as every man's being independent. The stars of heaven are all under law, each influencing the other to do the will of God, yielding their common obedience to the law that controls their action. And, in order that the Lord's work may advance healthfully and solidly, His people must draw together.[12]

Again, this testimony was sent in 1909. In spite of the ups, downs, twists, and turns that had occurred inside Adventism during earlier years, even at that late date the Lord's messenger still stated that there should be "no breaking down of the system of organization and order that has been built up by wise, careful labor." Instead of acting like Lucifer who chose a "spirit of independence" in heaven, "His people must draw together." This was the clear message of the Spirit of Prophecy. And again: The context of the paragraphs quoted above is the importance of God's people drawing together *inside the organized Seventh-day Adventist Church* whose leaders had gathered for a General Conference in 1909.

Unfortunately, many who accept teachings 1–3 summarized above take the next fearful step of no longer seeking to "draw together" inside the organized Seventh-day Adventist

---

12. *Testimonies for the Church*, vol. 9, pp. 257, 258 (emphasis added)

Church. Instead, they pull apart, cease returning their tithes to their local Adventist church and conference, leave the church, and even worse, they often pull others away from the church.

Consider this. In heaven:

1. Lucifer refused to submit to God's authority.

2. He spread discontent about God's leadership among angels.

3. He raised up a rebellious army in an attempt to take over.

Can't we see how, working behind the scenes, our ancient foe is craftily doing the same thing today in his war against the Godhead and God's organized Remnant Church? Speaking of the Godhead, the Heavenly Trio also recognizes authority. The Father gives authority to His Son (John 5:22, 27; Matt. 28:18); the Son submits to the authority of His Father (John 5:19; 6:38; 1 Cor. 11:3); and the Holy Spirit only speaks and teaches what He receives from the Father and His Son (John 16:13, 14). We also are to submit to the authority of all Three (Matt. 28:19, 20; Heb. 5:9; Rom. 8:14). Thus, submission to authority is how the Godhead run Their universe. If we don't learn the lesson of humbly submitting to authority, we run the risk of finally being cast into the lake of fire with the devil and his wicked angels (see Matt. 25:41; Rev. 20:10) who first rebelled against God's just authority and government in heaven.

Is the Adventist Church a perfect church? Hardly. Jesus declared it would be a mixture of both wise and foolish virgins (see Matt. 25:1–13), of both wheat and weeds (Matt. 13:36–43). Nevertheless, Mrs. White wrote:

When men arise, claiming to have a message from God, but instead of warring against principalities and powers, and the rulers of the darkness of this world, they form a hollow square, *and turn the weapons of warfare against the church militant, be afraid of them. They do not bear the divine credentials.* God has not given them any such burden of labor. They would tear down that which God would restore by the Laodicean message. He wounds only that He may heal, not cause to perish. The Lord lays upon no man a message that will discourage and dishearten the church.[13]

This is God's evaluation of those who are now fighting against the church militant by their speeches, articles, websites, and videos. "They do not bear the divine credentials," warns the Spirit of God. Following in the steps of Lucifer,

Instead of the unity which should exist among believers, there is disunion; for Satan is permitted to come in, and through his specious deceptions and delusions he leads *those who are not learning of Christ meekness and lowliness of heart, to take a different line from the church, and break up, if possible, the unity of the church.* Men arise speaking perverse things to draw away disciples after themselves. They claim that God has given them great light; but how do they act under its influence? Do they pursue the course that the two disciples pursued on their journey to Emmaus? When they received light, they returned and found

13. *Testimonies to Ministers*, p. 22 (emphasis added)

those whom God had led and was still leading, and told them how they had seen Jesus and had talked with Him.[14]

Therefore a key to avoiding Satan's snares is learning meekness and humility. In heaven, God showed Lucifer his errors, and where his terrible rebellion would take him—into coldness, darkness, and death. This mighty angel even realized he was wrong. Then he *almost* decided to return to his former submission to the authority of the Father and His Son. *"But pride forbade him.* It was too great a sacrifice for one who had been so highly honored to confess that he had been in error, that his imaginings were false, and to yield to the authority which he had been working to prove unjust."[15]

Something similar happened to Dr. Kellogg. After receiving merciful testimonies pointing out his errors, this verdict was pronounced: "You did not humble your heart, and confess, and become converted."[16] Instead, he allowed a "spirit of contention," and "a spirit of self-

---

14. *Ibid.*, p. 48 (emphasis added)
15. *Patriarchs and Prophets*, p. 39 (emphasis added)
16. *Special Testimonies,* Series B, Vol. 7, p. 46

exaltation," to rule within his soul.[17] Following in Lucifer's footsteps, in essence, Kellogg's pride ruined him. This is the same battle we all must fight. "He who has an ear, let him hear what the Spirit says to the churches." Revelation 2:11

"But the church is so sinful!" many claim. "We must leave it!" If Satan has been tempting you with this idea, realize that he presented similar arguments to sinless angels in heaven; and unfortunately, many fell under his strong delusions. This made them devils. If Satan is tempting you with similar arguments, consider this:

> Although *there are evils existing in the church,* and will be until the end of the world, the church in these last days is to be the light of the world that is polluted and demoralized by sin. The church, *enfeebled and defective, needing to be reproved, warned, and counseled, is the only object upon earth upon which Christ bestows His supreme regard.*[18]

---

17. *Ibid,* p. 55
18. *Testimonies to Ministers,* p. 49 (emphasis added)

Jesus loves His church (see Eph. 5:25), even though it is "enfeebled and defective." He wants us to love it, too. Just to be clear: yes, often we can't help but see *"evils existing in the church"* that should be addressed; and yes, sometimes even church leaders make wrong decisions which result in their "needing to be reproved, warned, and counseled." At such times faithful church members should always remember to put the Bible first (a Protestant principle), to "obey God rather than men" (Acts 5:29), and to pray for their leaders that God will help them. But even during times of turmoil, stress, and confusion, the church is *still* "the only object upon earth upon which Christ bestows His supreme regard."

As stated earlier, the Heavenly Trio raised up the Seventh-day Adventist Church and gave it a mission to spread the Three Angels' Messages worldwide to counteract the devil's satanic trio of the dragon, the beast, and the false prophet (see Rev. 16:14). In order to fully accomplish its holy, end-time mission, God's Church must remain organized.

This message has come to us in plain language:

When anyone is drawing apart from *the*

organized body of God's commandment-keeping people, when he begins to weigh the church in his human scales and begins to pronounce judgment against them, *then you may know that God is not leading him. He is on the wrong track.*[19]

"Wrong track" means just that: *"wrong track."*

It's time to get on the right track.

Let me tell you my personal story.

In 1979, I was a 20-year-old disco-dancing, marijuana-smoking, cocaine-snorting lost Jew living in California. One morning at my dad's house, I randomly turned on the TV set, and there was Pastor George Vandeman, Director of It is Written Television, which is still a ministry of the North American Division of Seventh-day Adventists. Holding an open Bible, Pastor Vandeman talked about the Bible Sabbath. His words gripped me. "Call the 800 number on the screen," he said kindly, looking straight at me, "and we'll send you a free copy of my book, *A Day to Remember.*"

At that moment an unseen power (the Third Person of the Godhead) tugged on my heart.

---

19. *Selected Messages*, vol. 3, p. 18 (emphasis added)

Call that number, was the impression of the Holy Spirit. I did. Unknown to me at the time, the phone rang at Andrews University, where I would later attend its Seminary. I ordered that book, which arrived at my dad's house a few days later. I read it in one sitting. Soon God led me to walk into the Canoga Park Seventh-day Adventist Church, a constituent church of the Southern California Adventist Conference. That day I met Pastor JB Church, who handed to me a copy of the book, *The Desire of Ages,* printed by Pacific Press. After reading that book, I gave my heart to Jesus, was baptized, and began taking classes at La Sierra College in preparation for the gospel ministry.

That was nearly 44 years ago.

This past August (2023) I attended the annual ASI Convention in Kansas City, MO, as a representative of White Horse Media, the ministry I work for. There, I visited with leaders who work for 3ABN, Amazing Facts, Secrets Unsealed, Remnant Publications, Life-Talk Radio, Adventist World Radio, Glow, and the Ellen G. White Estate. I also had a chance to visit with Ted Wilson, our current General Conference President. What a blessing to meet with these leaders involved in the worldwide work of God!

During one presentation in the main auditorium, a short video entitled, "Empty Shoes," was shown based on two empty shoes discovered floating in a Philippine Ocean after a helicopter carrying Adventist missionaries unexpectedly crashed into the sea. The empty shoes belonged to Janelle Alder. The video was a tribute to her sacrifice and appealed to others to bravely fill her shoes as missionaries. After that video, Elder Wilson made a stirring appeal to a large crowd. "Who will dedicate a year of your life to mission service?" Many walked forward indicating their decision.

It was a powerful moment.

The Holy Spirit was definitely present.

Unfortunately, many who have chosen the path of independence from the organized Seventh-day Adventist Church weren't at ASI. They generally don't attend such conferences, nor do they cooperate with the mainstream Adventist Church to fulfill God's mission. Somewhat like the "Essenes" in New Testament times who separated from Judaism to live in the desert, they also have separated from God's organized work. They think they are right. They are hard to convince otherwise. The Essenes thought they were the faithful few, too, yet their group isn't mentioned even once in the entire New Testament.

Recently I watched a video where a prominent member of the OTG movement frankly admitted that those who hold OTG teachings are scattered and disorganized. Some believe one thing, and some another. Some keep the feasts, while others believe in a flat earth. Many don't know where to send their tithes. Many OTG churches also don't get along with each other, he stated sadly, and some hardly talk to each other.

To me, they seem like wounded sheep without a shepherd.[20]

Our compassionate Redeemer declares:

On this Rock I will build My church, and the gates of Hades shall not prevail against it. Matthew 16:18

As a shepherd seeks out his flock on the day he is among his scattered sheep, so will I seek out My sheep and deliver them from all the places where they

---

20. For additional information about the problems with this movement, read "Why Anti-Trinitarianism is Not a Spirit-led Movement," by Rob Durkin, viewable at https://theheavenlytrio .com/antitrin.

were scattered on a cloudy and dark day.
Ezekiel 34:12

And I, if I am lifted up from the earth, will
draw all peoples to Myself. John 12:32

In these closing hours, our Savior wants
us to build our lives on His Word above all
human opinions. He also wants us to focus
on our mission, which is to share His Three
Angels' Messages worldwide and *lift Him up*
before "all peoples." Lost souls around the
world need to focus their minds on Jesus, on
His love, on His full Divinity, on His great
Sacrifice for our sins, and on His mighty
power "to save to the uttermost those who
come to God through Him." Heb. 7:25. Our
wonderful Savior must be lifted higher and
higher, not brought down lower and lower.

King Jesus loves us. His majesty is inde-
scribable. As we saw earlier, when He walked
this earth, "The whole ocean of divine love
was flowing forth from its great center. *The
Godhead—the Father, the Son, and the Holy
Spirit—were working in behalf of man.*"[21]

---

21. *Letters and Manuscripts*, vol. 16, Manuscript 47, 1901
(emphasis added)

Wow! The entire Godhead, and Jesus specifically, is the "great center" for an "ocean of divine love" to flow to human hearts. What a marvelous thought! By His Holy Spirit, Jesus longs to convict us of sin, soften our hearts, and change our lives.

In this Day of Atonement, we should humble ourselves, and confess our own sins, rather than dwelling on the defects of others. "Instead of finding fault with others [a trait of the Pharisees], let us be critical with ourselves."[22] This is not the time to become endlessly engaged in divisive debates about the Godhead. If we don't exactly see eye to eye on small points, we should be charitable to each other. My wife Kristin and I don't see every issue in life exactly alike either, but we still love each other, and we are still happily married.

Shortly before Pentecost, Christ's disciples who had so often bickered and argued about which one was greatest, committed themselves to drawing together. "Putting away all differences, all desire for the supremacy, they came close together in Christian fellowship."[23]

22. *Review and Herald,* Feb. 25, 1904
23. *Acts of the Apostles,* p. 37

Then the Holy Spirit was poured out like a rushing mighty wind.

We can follow their example. Coming together, we can unitedly cooperate with the Father, His Son, and the Holy Spirit in Their loving and unselfish efforts to finish Their work so we can go home to a better land.

When I first read *The Desire of Ages* about the life of Jesus Christ, I read about His miracles, His love for the lost, His tender patience with open sinners, His agonizing struggle in Gethsemane, His death on a cruel cross for my sins, His quiet rest in a silent grave, He glorious resurrection, and His ascension to heaven.

That's what changed my heart. "No more drugs for me!" I finally decided. In a dormitory room at California State University of Northridge, I then knelt down for the first time in my life and asked Jesus to become my Lord and Savior. He heard my prayer! After nearly 44 years, I'm still holding onto Him by faith and looking forward to His soon return.

At the conclusion of this book I appeal *to you,* dear reader, to focus your mind *on Jesus,* on the importance of unity, and on fulfilling our divine mission. In spite of its faults, don't abandon God's Church, and don't divide it either. Determine also not to be among those who "generate strife." 2 Tim. 2:23. "Press together, press together!" Ellen White pleaded, "In union there is strength and victory; in discord and division there is weakness and defeat. *These words have been spoken to me from heaven. As God's ambassador I speak them to you.*"[24]

"If anyone has an ear, let him hear." Revelation 13:9

Like the early disciples, the calling of Seventh-day Adventists is to "Go" and "make disciples of all the nations, baptizing them in the name of the Father and of the Son and of the Holy Spirit." Matt. 28:19. Our work is to communicate the Three Angels' Messages worldwide, and we must be united to do it. At the heart of these messages is "the everlasting gospel" (Rev. 14:6) about our Lord Jesus Christ, His Divine Person, His love, His law, His gift of Righteousness, His grace, His infinite sacrifice on that cruel cross for our wicked sins, His resurrection, and His glorious return.

Let's remain focused.

Let's kneel low at the foot of His cross.

The Father, the Son, and the Holy Spirit are calling us.

---

24. *Testimonies for the Church*, vol. 5, p. 488 (emphasis added)

Each of Them care deeply about us, for "God is love." 1 John 4:8

Satan and his infernal forces are still heartlessly warring against the Godhead and Their organized Seventh-day Adventist Church—but they will lose. By God's grace, armed with the mighty weapons of His Holy Word, let's resist their deceptions. "It is written," our Savior said, "Man shall not live by bread alone, but by every word that proceeds out of the mouth of God." Matt. 4:4

Shortly before He suffered in Gethsemane and on Calvary, Jesus prayed earnestly to His Father that His disciples "may be one, as We are." John 17:11. Just think of it! Just as the mighty "Us" first mentioned in the beginning of the Bible have eternally been united in "one" mind, character, and purpose, even so does the same Heavenly Trio want us to become "one" with each other (as much as possible) in these last days of earth's history.

The Three Angels are not divided.

Neither should we be as we proclaim God's messages.

Recently an awful fire destroyed the town of Lahaina, on the island of Maui. In one news report, the mayor was quoted as saying, "This is a time for us to come together. This is the time for us to care for each other in our county." Surely these words also apply to each member of God's Seventh-day Adventist Remnant Church of Bible Prophecy.

If we love Jesus, we will seek to answer His prayer.

I'll close with this inspired appeal from His servant Paul:

I, therefore, the prisoner of the Lord, beseech you to walk worthy of the calling with which you were called, with all lowliness and gentleness, with longsuffering, bearing with one another in love, *endeavoring to keep the unity of the Spirit in the bond of peace.* Ephesians 4:1–3 (emphasis added)

THE END

To learn more about the Godhead,
White Horse Media recommends:

The Trinity Controversy
[5-part series on White Horse Media's
YouTube Channel and on DVD]

Understanding the Godhead:
My Personal Journey
By Joel Ridgeway
[Book]

Missionary Resources by Steve Wohlberg
to Help You and Your Church Spread
God's Three Angels' Messages:

New! *Messages from Heaven*
[Small sharing tract explaining
the Three Angels' Messages]

God's Final Warning:
The Three Angels' Messages
[Pocketbook]

The Truth about the Sabbath:
Discover Proof That the Seventh-day
(Saturday) Is Still God's Holy Day
[Pamphlet]

False Prophecies about Israel,
Babylon, and Armageddon

Decoding the Mark of the Beast

End Times Health War

The Coming Judgments of God

The United States in Bible Prophecy

Climate Change:
Is It the End of the World?

Is God's Church Built on Peter?

Hidden Holocaust:
Discover God's Love
in the Abortion Nightmare

The Character of God Controversy

God Speaks Before the End of the World
[Explains the prophetic ministry of Ellen
White]

Will My Pet Go to Heaven?

Help for the Hopeless

White Horse Media Television Series
(Viewable on its YouTube Channel
and available on DVD)

God: Fact or Fiction?
Weighing the Evidence

The Abortion Controversy:
Two Women Tell Their Stories of Hope and
Healing

Coming Out:
Former Gays Testify of God's Saving Love

Body Battles:
Protect Your Health. Avoid Dying Early.

Finding Hope in Depression and Despair

Preparation for the End-Times

Is Jesus Kosher for Jews?

Good News for Muslims

God, Satan, Money, and YOU

The Elijah Prophecy

Dark Waters:
Finding Hope in Tragedy

Available From:

White Horse Media
P.O. Box 130
Priest River, Idaho 83856
1-800-782-4253
www.whitehorsemedia.com

Sign up for Steve Wohlberg's free
e-newsletter at: www.whitehorsemedia.com

Follow him on Twitter:
@WhiteHorse7

Find him on Facebook:
www.facebook.com/stevewohlberg